A GARDENING GUIDE

STARRING

SLUGS DEER SQUIRRELS MOLES MICE
CATS BIRDS FOXES SHEEP & RABBITS

THIRD EDITION

Published
October 2002

Printed in Glasgow

COMMON
GARDEN ENEMIES

Janet Thomson

CONTENTS

For

David and Harry Young

INTRODUCTION

This is a book for all those who suffer relentless damage by garden enemies and simply do not know where to turn. It is also for gardeners who have battled against their enemies, sometimes winning but often wondering what to do next. One thing is clear: none of these uninvited species is ever going to disappear and so we have to learn how to live with them.

Much has been written about bugs and diseases and so these are not the subject of this book. Rather, it is the larger, more awkward enemies which will be exposed, dissected and dealt with in the following pages. Slugs, deer, squirrels, moles, mice, cats, birds, foxes, sheep and rabbits all come under the microscope.

Those happy people, successful gardeners, have found ways of managing invaders therefore limiting the damage. Not for them howls of self pity and cries of 'why me?!' Just good old trial-and-error gardening to see what works for them and ask what has worked for others.

Since the answer to a problem often lies in a different way of looking at it, this book encourages the gardener to be assertive and go out there to find a solution rather than waste energy wishing the enemy would just disappear.

Janet Thomson
November, 1998

FOREWORD

A weed is described as a plant in the wrong place. The same could be said of the stars of this book.
That's realism.

In my experience, I have met people who like slugs! Quote: 'I would like you to suggest how I might clear slugs from my garden, but I wouldn't like them to come to any harm.'
That's cowardice.

There is no doubt in my mind that all-out war must be waged, even although you may have to take a defensive stance from time to time. Have you tried compromise? Have you tried to share a plate of tatties and mince by the campfire with a swarm of flies? I have and they won't stick to their side of the plate.
That's politics.

Have you met someone who has just lost the young growth on their prize roses to the local bunch of B..........ambis? Take my advice: don't even think of asking if they managed to get a good picture. Have you experienced that sense of frustration and despair at the sight of Mr Mole having taken the Metro route across your otherwise immaculate lawn? Why couldn't he have taken the surface route like the rest of us?
That's just being a human being seriously considering atheism!

See me, see rabbits..........ugh.....***.....!!

This book will be welcomed by many; like aspirin it will help the pain - rejoice at the short term respite!

Jim McColl MBE

1
COMMON ENEMIES:
Slugs &Vertebrates

Gardening is undoubtedly one of life's greatest pleasures which is enjoyed by an increasing number of people. Although most gardeners are too sensible to expect their pleasures to be completely hassle-free, there are certain irritations which can prove a little too much for all but the most stalwart. These are the gardening enemies within.

Slugs, snails, deer, squirrels, moles, birds, cats, mice, foxes, sheep and rabbits are all guilty of annoying gardeners. The most prevalent of these is the slug from whom few can escape. Foxes and sheep, although less common, can also provoke the most placid person to dole out punishment. True to the old Scots motto, *'Nemo me impune lacessit'* or *'Wha daur meddle wi' me!'* is the battle cry as the irate gardener exchanges hoe for arms and vows to fight back.

It is important that not only should the punishment fit the crime but that any measures taken should work. The key to defeating common garden enemies lies in knowing their weaknesses. In Greek mythology, Achilles was the famous warrior who fought against the Trojans. As a child, his mother dipped him into the river Styx to make him immortal. However, she held him by the heel and so this spot remained vulnerable all his life. At the battle of Troy, Achilles was mortally wounded in the heel by Paris.

Each animal is therefore subjected to close scrutiny and his 'Achilles heel' exposed for all to see. Armed with this knowledge, the artful gardener can freely experiment and improvise to discover ever more subtle techniques to outwit his enemy.

Although much can be done to protect plants and even discourage the enemy from our soil, it is important to guard against unrealistic expectations. Aim to strike a balance where gardener and enemy may co-exist, avoiding the temptation to wage such an all-out war that the garden becomes nothing more than a gory battlefield. After all, who would want to win a *Pyrrhic victory?

The following pages contain many valuable gems of ideas, both old and new, to tackle the most stubborn adversary. Gardens should be enjoyed. Rather than allow the unwelcome intruder to spoil our fun, we might derive even more pleasure if we accept the challenge and win.

*Continuing the ancient Greek theme, Pyrrhus, King of Epirus, gave his name to the unhappy condition 'Pyrrhic victory'. With his army of 25,000 men and 20 elephants, he won the battle against the Romans but at such a huge cost that it was questionable whether the victory was worthwhile at all.

2
EXPOSING THE SLUG

The slug who prefers to be known by his Sunday title 'terrestrial gastropod mollusc' is the most ubiquitous of gardeners' enemies. The four inch (10 cm) long European great grey slug was introduced into North America where he pursues his career with joyous abandon.

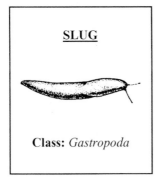

SLUG

Class: *Gastropoda*

A wander through any garden by day would prompt the unwary to question the slug's lofty position in gardening enemy lists. However, a sneaky reconnoitre through the garden with a torch on a warm, damp evening will quickly reduce most human legs to quivering jelly.

Dozens of these 'belly-footed' animals can be found wending their way through the garden leaving behind tell-tale trails of slime secreted from a gland on the underside of their soft bodies. Slugs themselves are also covered in this mucus which prevents dehydration and inspires long-suffering gardeners with ideas for dealing with this nocturnal intruder.

Grey and fawn slugs do most damage to plants. Amongst the twenty types of slug in this country is the dark-brown one with a lump on its back who has a penchant for underground tubers and bulbs. The gloriously sleek black slugs (6 inches/15 cm long) are not so keen on mature plants but love seedlings.

Projecting from the mouth opening is the radula or ribbon-like tongue which contains thousands of minute teeth or denticles. These are drawn across the plant in a rasping motion as leaves, stems, flowers, tubers and bulbs are reduced to a sludgy fodder.

After a long night gorging himself at our expense, the sated slug crawls back under a stone to slumber in solitude and dream of feasts to come. Stones are not the only hiding place sought by slugs: any garden debris can act as shelter.

Tell-tale signs of slug damage are most likely to be seen near ground level. Holes in flowers, stems and leaves as well as cavities in potato tubers and bulbs signal the busy slug. High on their favourite menu are seedlings, dead leaves, hosta, delphinium, anemone, coreopsis, lilies, gerbera, helenium, hyacinth, dahlia, daffodils, narcissi, iris, lupins, rudbeckia, primula, sweet peas, tulips, lobelia erinus, violas, pansies and vegetables.

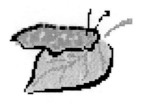

Different types of slug breed at different times of the year. Being hermaphrodites, they self-fertilise and so all slugs can lay eggs. Gardeners should keep a sharp look-out for small, round, soft eggs around 1/8 inch (3mm) in diameter and get rid of them before they have a chance to hatch (usually in warm, damp conditions). Digging over the ground exposes the eggs.

3
CONTROL AND OUTWIT THE SLUG

 While it can be satisfying to take the law into the sole of your own boot, there are many more subtle options for controlling the slug. The most obvious is a thorough tidy-up, removing debris to an area of garden where you might wish to encourage natural predators.

Provide an area with long grass, ground-covering plants or log piles where frogs, toads, hedgehogs and ground beetles might hide. Be wary of feeding hedgehogs so well that they prefer your food to a humble diet of slug!

Hoe or fork the soil in the borders and vegetable garden to bring the slug to the surface where he can be picked off by birds or dried out by sun and wind. Water plants in the morning so the soil is not too damp at night. Grow plants in sunny spots and away from hiding places. Grow seedlings in trays and transplant some into pots to keep as backup for those which might perish in the garden.

Healthy plants are better able to recover from slug damage and may even attract fewer slugs since they prefer damaged and decaying material. Be prepared to treat damaged plants which might succumb to fungal disease. Spores can develop in slime trails and lodge in plants through wounds made by browsing slugs.

One of the craftiest ways to outwit slugs is simply to grow plants which they don't much fancy (see list on page 16). Although the hosta is the first plant which springs to mind when slugs are mentioned, *hosta tardiflora* with its leathery foliage is said to be resistant to slug damage. Hostas and other vulnerable plants can also be grown in tubs where you can keep an eye on them.

Lettuce varieties *Lollo Rosso* and *Lollo Verdi* are also reported as being repulsive not only to slugs but also to insects and fungi. Their extremely crinkled leaves may have something to do with this unexpected trait.

In late summer when other plants are dying back, the slug will sometimes turn his attention to potatoes. Trim leaves to prevent them resting on the ground since slugs will quickly find their way from the leaves to the tubers. Rotting burrows and cavities mean slugs are busy and so vulnerable tubers should be lifted early and stored.

Vulnerable types include: *Desiree, Glade, King Edward, Maris Piper, Pentland Crown, Record* and *Redskin.* It could be worth experimenting with varieties such as *Pentland Dell, Pentland Squire* and *Majestic.* Sow *Accent* and *Foremost* which are better able to resist slug damage.

Many young vegetables, for example lettuce and cabbage, do require protection from slugs. One method is to cradle each one in a piece of plastic milk container cut open and fitted between vegetable and soil.

Germinate runner beans inside until the seedlings are large enough to withstand slug damage. When seeds require to be sown directly into soil, finely rake the ground then cover the site with polythene and allow to dry for a few days. Make seed drill and water the bottom only. Sow seeds, cover with dry soil and protect seedlings with a cloche.

Encourage the slug away from your plants and towards a nice mulch of manure or organic matter. He is especially happy on wet, clay soil, while autumn and spring rain only serves to make his life easier.

 Keep chickens or ducks! They will gobble up slugs although they also tend to enjoy the odd scratch around in your flower beds.

A favourite tactic is to remove slugs during day from under stones and debris or to go out at night with a torch and pick them off the ground. The prisoners can then be removed to a distant cabbage field or similar slug haven. Some harsh individuals will drop the slugs into an empty can then pour boiling water on them for a quick death.

A variation on this mediaeval treatment is to tip the poor creatures into a bucket of concentrated salt solution. Salt may also be shaken from a salt cellar directly onto the slug's body. This will dry out his mucus glands, making it impossible for him to move to shelter in the morning. He will then be vulnerable from attack by predators and at risk from the drying effects of the sun.

Sounding just as cruel is the sprinkler method where slugs are sprayed with a 50:50 solution of water and vinegar.

Never in a thousand years could we banish slugs from the garden, so we really should not resort to such despotic methods, but should instead practise some of those crafty diversionary tactics discussed in the next two sections.

*

Age-Old Slug Remedies

The golden rules in the war against slugs are roughness, dryness and drowning. Commence battle armed with the least cruel of the following tried-and-tested remedies. If desperate, scale up to serious warfare, spending money where necessary.

1. *The Beer Trap*

Sink a plastic cup into the soil every few feet near base of plant so the rim is at ground level. Half-fill with beer and wait. Empty the cup (not a pleasant task!) and replace every two or three nights. If frogs eat drunken slugs they might themselves succumb to alcoholic poisoning, so you might prefer to try milk which can also be used to soak newspapers that you leave overnight on the soil. Next morning simply take the papers loaded underneath with slugs and place them in the bin.

2. *Grapefruit Skins*

Upturned grapefruit skins can be used as a trap for slugs. Once caught, the slug can be transported to a site of your choice. Cabbage leaves, wet newspapers, tiles and stones can also be placed in strategic positions and examined periodically for lurking slugs.

3. *Milk Carton Cloche*

Cut the top and bottom from empty milk cartons and slip over seedlings for overnight protection. Cardboard tubing from toilet rolls, short bits of plastic drainpipe or pieces cut from a plastic soft drink bottle would serve the same purpose.

4. *Rough and Dry Mulches*

Let your imagination run wild and experiment. Successful materials include: *sharp gravel; sharp sand; cocoa shells; bark; soot; wood ash; crushed eggshells; hair clippings; slaked lime; pine needles; old sacking.*

When the slug encounters these unexpected textures around the base of plants, his usual reaction will be to change direction. Slugs require smooth, moist surfaces in order to move around and so the above are most effective when dry and should be replaced after rain.

5. *Slippery Pots*

 Cut out the base of a small plastic pot (e.g. yoghurt carton), cover pot in boot polish and place over small plant. Slugs will find it impossible to crawl up the side of the pot.

6. *Comfrey Leaves*

It has been said that if Comfrey leaves are spread around the base of a plant, slugs will leave the plant alone. This remedy only seems to work before midsummer!

7. *Herbal Tea*

Sprinkle southernwood or wormwood tea over soil in spring and autumn.

Depending on factors such as soil type, weather and plant varieties, some of the above solutions should make a difference in the garden. However, more help is at hand for those still suffering from this scourge of nature. The following items are commercially available and should easily be found at the local garden centre.

Biology & Technology

1. *Nematodes*

The nematode *Phasmarhabditis hermaphrodita* is a microscopic worm which normally lives in the soil. Supplied in a powdered clay base directly from the producer, this parasite (which can be refrigerated in sealed packets for four weeks) is activated when water is added. The solution is sprayed onto the soil from where the nematodes enter through pores in the slug's skin. Bacteria are released, poisoning the slug which stops eating and dies a few days later.

Having multiplied inside the slug, many more nematodes move into the soil and parasitise more slugs. Earthworms are not affected, nor can the nematode harm pets and people thanks to our relatively high body temperature. The treatment lasts for six weeks and is usually applied between March and October.

2. *Slug Pellets*

Pellets based on methiocarb or metaldehyde are spread thinly (3-6 inches/7.5-15cm apart) on the soil and are eaten by slugs. Since metaldehyde accumulates in the slug's body, predators could be killed or harmed if they then eat the slugs. Pellets contain a repellent to prevent them being eaten by pets and are dyed blue to make them unattractive to birds. The safest way to use slug pellets is to place them under tiles or slates or bury them in shallow seed drills. They must be reapplied following heavy rain which makes them ineffective.

3. Slug Crystals

Crystals based on aluminium sulphate remain effective for four days and are not harmful to other creatures. These contain no poison and simply dry out the slug's slime organs thus preventing him from moving around and feeding. Rain or dampness can rehydrate the slug. Avoid contact with young plants since the salt dries out cells and kills leaves. Use liquid aluminium sulphate or liquid metaldehyde for those small slugs which live in the soil and attack tubers. Herbs and vegetables cannot be picked for eating for ten days after spraying the ground.

4. Electric Fence

An electric slug fence can be purchased as a barrier between slug and flower border. Made of black plastic the 6 inch (15 cm) high fence is pegged into the ground and its two wires attached to a 12 volt battery.

5. Pit Fall

Partially submerge a beer trap (covered to keep out rain) in the soil and bait with beer, yeast tablets (which last longer than beer) or lettuce leaves.

6. Slug Jail

The slug jail is filled with barley, rice or yeast to attract slugs which, once inside, are unable to escape. The jail protects up to 50 sq feet (4.65 sq m).

7. Granules, Grit and Spray

Proprietary granules, grit and spray can be bought.

8. Snail-proof Saucer

Battery-powered plant pot saucer gives slugs a small electric shock, enough to send them on their way.

Thankfully there are plants which seem to remain unpopular with the slug. Below is a list of some of those voted out of the slugs' good food guide - voted out with their gastropods, presumably.

27 *PLANTS WHICH SLUGS TEND TO AVOID*

*A*conitum napellus (**Monkshood**)
Althaea rosea (**Hollyhock**)
Antirrhinum majus (**Snapdragon**)

*C*alendula officinalis (**Marigold**)
Cheiranthus cheiri (**Wallflower**)
Cistus purpurius (**Rock Rose**)
Cosmos bipinnatus

*D*ianthus barbatus (**Sweet William**)
Diascia

*E*chinacea purpurea (**Purple Cone Flower**)
Echinops ritro (**Globe Thistle**)

*F*uchsia (**Hardy Shrub Fuchsia**)

*G*eranium (**Perennial Geranium**)
Godetia

*H*ebe pinguifolia (**Veronica**)
Helichrysum (**Straw flower**)
Hosta tardiflora (<u>not</u> other hostas!)

*L*athyrus odoratus (**Sweet Pea**)
Lavandula angustifolia (**Lavender**)
Lavatera trimestris (**Mallow**)
Lobularia maritima (**Sweet Alyssum**)

*P*apaver rhoeas (**Poppy**)
Penstemon campanulatus (**Penstemon**)
Primula (**Polyanthus**)

*S*tachys byzantina (**Lamb's Tongue**)

*T*ropaeolum majus (**Nasturtium**)

*V*erbascum (**Mullein**)

ACHILLES HEEL OF THE SLUG

DISLIKES DRY SURFACES

DISLIKES ROUGH SURFACES

DRIED-OUT MUCUS GLANDS

4

NOT FORGETTING THE SNAIL

In case that other infamous gastropod, the snail, thinks he can escape our attentions, a few words should be said about his contribution to garden warfare. A foraging snail also enjoys a meal of our plants and should be given the same treatment as his cousin.

Snails have prominent tentacles with eyes on the end and move along in the same way as slugs. Whereas a slug's shell is represented by a mere internal horny plate which overlies the respiratory cavity, snails glory in a wonderfully decorative armoured coat. Not only does the shell protect the snail from predators, it also prevents him from drying out in the sun and wind. Snails tend to hibernate from late October until spring. They usually mate at night in late spring and their eggs hatch in 25 days.

Sadly, the decline of the song thrush population denies many of us the entertainment of seeing this natural predator getting to grips with a tasty meal. Taking the snail in its beak, the thrush will toss its head from side to side, hitting its prey against a favourite stone until its shell cracks open. Once the soft body of the snail is exposed,

the thrush makes short work of devouring a well-earned feed. The loud 'tap-tapping' of shell on stone used to be a familiar sound in gardens and woodlands.

Take comfort in knowing that snail droppings make excellent organic fertiliser which is good for lettuces!

It has been estimated that up to 50 slugs and snails can occupy one square metre of garden soil. One experiment removed 27,500 from a small garden with no noticeable lowering of activity! It is hopeless to attempt to eradicate them and so gardeners can only do their best to protect young vegetables and herbaceous plants, strawberries and seedlings. Since they are such good scavengers of decaying organic material, we should try to respect their contribution to the ecology of our gardens.

It's always worth trying to discover features of a plant which the enemy doesn't like. Make a note of plants which remain undamaged and stock up with plenty of similar types. Be liberal in planting trees and shrubs since they will not be harmed by slugs and snails. Acidic garden soil should be less popular with snails since they prefer alkaline soil from which they obtain lime to build shells.

*

The rain stops.
The air is sprung with green.
The intercepted drops
Fall at their leisure; and between
The threading runnels on the slopes
The snail drags his caution into the sun.

Christopher Fry
Rain on Dry Ground

5
EXPOSING THE DEER

The first deer appeared in Asia 38 million years ago and are now found also in Europe, America and Africa. Inhabiting mainly wooded areas and open land, deer feed on bushes, leaves, bark, saplings, buds, grass and other plants. They are most active in the evening when they fill up with food which is digested in a four-chambered stomach. Being ruminants, they also chew the cud.

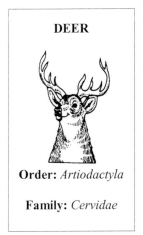

DEER

Order: *Artiodactyla*

Family: *Cervidae*

Their ability to consume a wide variety of vegetation is due in part to the grinding motion of lower cheek teeth which are coated with crescent ridges of enamel. Deer are fleet of foot and able to cover large distances in a short time. The design of their toes makes it easy for them to cross rocky ground and gives them their splendid title: artiodactyl mammal.

There are six different species of deer in the UK including *Capreolus Capreolus*, the roe deer and the larger *Cervus Dama*, the fallow deer, both of which are gaining quite a reputation for damaging the environment. *Cerphus Elaphus* is the famous red deer, indigenous to the UK. North American species include elk, mule deer and white tail deer.

So long as deer remain in the wild, we are happy. However the sight of a wonderful set of antlers looming out of the twilight is becoming increasingly common. The lure of an easy meal helps them conquer shyness, bringing them ever closer to civilisation and into our gardens. We only have ourselves to blame for this, since in recent times we have ventured further and further into their traditional habitats.

Thankfully, gardeners' concerns are beginning to be taken seriously and damage by deer is now acknowledged to affect more than farmland and forests. The British Deer Society in Fordingbridge is a registered charity offering a wide range of information and support for research into deer issues.

As well as eating plants and shrubs, deer will strip bark from young trees. Wounds will be open to fungal infection while the tree could easily die or at least have its growth stunted. Shrubs and trees with frayed stems and branches should alert the gardener to deer activity especially in spring when the buck marks his territory. Deer leave a plant with shoots and stems which have been cut through cleanly on one side, with a frayed edge on the other.

In severe weather deer become hungry and bolder. It is best to use several methods of control since they may also learn to tolerate certain deterrents.

6
SURVIVING THE DEER

1. *Fence*

Gardeners troubled by deer have a very difficult time indeed. Some choose to build a fence 5 to 6 feet (1.5 to 1.8m) high around the garden. This solution, which is obviously unsuitable for many people, has to include deer-proof gates and driveways or even a cattle grid.

Deer are very good at finding their way under fences which can also be damaged by large deer. The small, secretive muntjac deer could easily squeeze through even a little hole in the fence. This option is expensive and should only be considered by gardeners able to carry out regular maintainance.

2. Tree Protectors

The bark of young trees must be protected by tree guards. Buy cylindrical plastic guards with perforations which prevent condensation and allow the tree to breathe or make your own from wire mesh.

3. Wire Mesh

Wire mesh can also be laid on the ground in an attempt to deter deer from crossing, but this is not always successful.

4. Lion Dung

People fortunate enough to live near a zoo could try spreading lion dung around the periphery of the garden. Since the lion is a predatory animal, he excretes a phenol compound in his urine which frightens off other animals. Clay pellets impregnated with liquidised lion dung are also commercially available. Pellets are irradiated therefore free from disease and are ecologically safe. North American gardeners might wish to try a variation on this theme: coyote urine. Deer also dislike being near dogs, probably for the same reason.

5. Deer Scarer

Garden centres supply bamboo deer scarers, driven by water which slowly fills the hollow, cylindrical shoot until it tips over. Such sudden noises and unexpected movement startle the deer. Gardeners handy with a saw might enjoy constructing their own version of this device.

6. *Gaudy Scarers*

Experiment with some home-made scarers of a more gaudy type, such as tinsel, tin cans or coloured rags and feathers strung across pathways and garden entrances. These are likely to be of use only in the short-term.

7. *Trip Wire*

Wire or twine stretched across routes known to be used by deer might upset them enough to make them turn back. However, care should be taken to avoid damage to other animals or humans!

8. *Woolly Protectors*

Wind lengths of wool around leading plant shoots, giving them a chance to grow out of reach of the deer.

9. *Electric Fence*

An electric cattle fence around the garden would be suitable in certain rural areas.

10. *Rotten Eggs*

The pungent smell of rotten eggs, or hydrogen sulphide, is exploited in a proprietary deer-repellent.

11. *Culinary Delights*

Throw a few unpalatable things into your kitchen blender to make a spray for favourite plants. Some success has been reported with a solution of chilli, hot pepper sauce and rotten eggs!

12. *Pepper Dust*

Dust plants with pepper or chilli powder, but be aware of possible damage to insects or the plant itself.

Plants which Deer Love

azalea   clematis   roses

rhododendron   mountain ash

fruit trees

Deer also Like

holly   forsythia   spiraea

hydrangea   cotoneaster

viburnum

Deer will eat many types of trees and plants, some of which are noted above.

Thankfully, there are certain plants which deer seem to shun (see list overleaf). Since deer tastes vary in different parts of the country, plant lists are therefore best used as guides and gardeners should experiment, customising the list to suit particular conditions.

*

The wild Deer wandering here and there
Keeps the Human Soul from Care.

William Blake
Auguries of Innocence

24 Plants which Deer Tend to Avoid

Anemone coronaria 'De Caen' (**Windflower**)
Antirrhinum majus (**Snapdragon**)

Berberis darwinii (**Barberry**)
Buddleja davidii (**Butterfly Bush**)
Buxus sempervirens (**Common Box**)

Calendula officinalis (**Marigold**)
Centaurea montana (**Mountain Knapweed**)
Chrysanthemum maximum (**Shasta Daisy**)
Cornus (**Dogwood**)

Dianthus barbatus (**Sweet William**)
Digitalis purpurea (**Common Foxglove**)

Lavandula angustifolia (**Lavender**)
Lysimachia punctata (**Yellow Loosestrife**)
Lythrum salicaria Robert (**Purple Loosestrife**)

Myosotis sylvatica (**Forget-me-not**)

Narcissus pseudonarcissus (**Wild Daffodil**)

Oenothera mossouriensis (**Evening Primrose**)

Papaver orientalis (**Oriental Poppy**)
Papaver rhoeas (**Field Poppy**)
Primula vulgaris (**Primrose**)

Rosmarinus (**Rosemary**)

Stachys byzantina olympus (**Lamb's Tongue**)
Syringia vulgaris (**Lilac**)

Vinca major (**Greater Periwinkle**)

In addition to the above plants, herbs such as chives, mint, oregano and sage may be grown in deer zones.

ACHILLES HEEL OF THE DEER

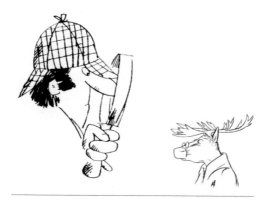

DISLIKES SUDDEN NOISE

DISLIKES SUDDEN MOVEMENT

SCARED OF PREDATORS

7
EXPOSING THE SQUIRREL

Squirrels are found all across the world except Australia. There are 230 species of tree and ground squirrel from Africa's 5 inch (13 cm) long pygmy squirrel to Asia's 36 inch (90 cm) long giant squirrel.

SQUIRREL

Order: *Rodentia*

Family: *Sciuridiae*

Sub-family: *Sciurinae*

Parks in North America are home to large numbers of grey squirrels, *Sciurus Carolinensis*. These have been introduced into the UK, resulting in a dramatic reduction in numbers of the smaller native red squirrel, *Sciurus Vulgaris* which cannot compete for food and habitat.

Contrary to popular belief, squirrels do not hibernate since they do not put on sufficient weight to sleep through winter. They must feed to keep energy levels high and they spend most of their time in trees. The grey squirrel is busy for around three hours each day in winter and feeds mainly at dawn. Eating mainly nuts, seeds and buds, squirrels will sometimes also include insects in their diet.

Female grey squirrels nest inside a hole in a tree where they rear litters of 3-6 young born in late winter or in summer. Their nest is called a 'drey'.

One of the first signs of squirrel activity is bark which has been stripped from stems and branches. Squirrels learn this habit of bark-stripping at an early age. Having dropped the outer bark, grey squirrels will eat the newly-exposed phloem tissue. Around mid-summer, trees are rich in phloem prior to lignification. This fluid contains sugars and it has been noticed that squirrels are more likely to damage trees with the greatest volume of sap. Trees with low sap volumes are mostly found in densely-planted areas but single trees with low sap volume also suffer less damage as the squirrel goes off to find more nourishment for his trouble.

When a tree is ring-barked low on the stem, it will die. Less extensive stripping encourages fungal infection and insect damage which at best stunt growth but can be fatal. Bulbs which have been dug up and disturbed soil (especially soft soil) also point to the presence of these attractive little rodents. They love to nibble new crocus shoots and eat bulbs.

Not least of the squirrels' annoying habits is that of stealing nuts and seeds lovingly provided to feed hungry garden birds during our long winters. Since they love dry places in which to relax, squirrels have been known to set up home in bird boxes - even sometimes in squirrel-proof boxes!

They will jump from tree to tree and so nut-bearing trees, e.g. hazel, should be planted at least 12 feet (3.6 m) away from other trees.

8
ANNOYING THE SQUIRREL

If large numbers of squirrels are suspected, people should never attempt to intervene but instead contact local environmental health officers who can remove their dreys.

1. *Tree Guards*

 Although little can be done to prevent squirrels tearing bark from trees, spiral protectors or plastic tree guards can be put around saplings to help them establish.

2. *Wire Mesh*

To protect bulbs, cover the area with wire mesh immediately after planting. Newly-dug soil simply alerts the squirrel to the possibility of a tasty meal.

3. *Chicken Wire*

Another use for wire mesh is to place it just below the surface of the soil to prevent young plants being uprooted. As the plants become established and you are sure they are safe from the squirrel, the wire can easily be snipped free.

4. *Prickly Branches*

Let Mr. Squirrel know he is not welcome by placing spiny or prickly branches on the ground. Rose, berberis and gorse cuttings should get your message across.

5. *Aquarium Gravel*

A thick mulch of aquarium gravel spread around flower beds, tubs and planters can be surprisingly effective.

6. *Ultrasound*

An electronic device which also wards off unwelcome cats and rabbits is placed in the garden. This sends out a high frequency ultrasound beam which is beyond the hearing range of most humans but is very annoying to the squirrel making him move away from the source of the sound. Birds are unaffected by this device.

7. *Helium-filled Balloons*

A child's balloon filled with helium and firmly tied to a stake in the ground will float and move around in the wind. Such a constantly-moving object tricks the squirrel into thinking there is a predator on the loose and so he is reluctant to risk entering the area.

8. *Cats and Dogs*

People with cats and dogs appear to suffer less from squirrels. Scent probably plays as great a part in this as the actual physical presence of the animal. But since squirrels will also learn to avoid unpleasant or dangerous situations and they dislike sudden movement, knowing that a cat or dog is likely to appear can be a wonderful deterrent.

9. *Permanent Planting*

Simple ideas are often the best and permanent planting of shrubs and perennials is one example. Since squirrels prefer to dig soft soil, this should be left undisturbed.

10. *Fruit Cages*

Commercially-available aluminium frames covered with plastic netting form cages used to keep birds away from fruit. These can be used to exclude squirrels from plantations of young trees.

11. *Birdseed Additive*

A preparation of capsicum peppers can be bought and added to birdseed, producing a hot chilli-like scent which squirrels detest. Other animals and birds don't mind this so seeds can be sprinkled on bird tables, pots etc. This can also be used in planters, in the soil to protect seedlings or sprinkled over bulbs.

12. *Squirrel-Proof Pole*

Keep squirrels off the bird table by fitting proprietary revolving discs and baffles on the pole.

*

> If we had a keen vision and feeling
> of all ordinary human life,
> it would be like hearing the grass grow
> and the squirrel's heart beat,
> and we should die of that roar
> which lies on the other side of silence.

George Eliot
From:
Middlemarch

32

ACHILLES HEEL OF THE SQUIRREL

DISLIKES SUDDEN MOVEMENT

DETESTS HOT TASTES

9
EXPOSING THE MOLE

There are twelve genera of mole including the American garden mole *scalopus* and the European *Talpa europaea*. This little mammal with rudimentary eyes, pointed snout, short legs and broad feet sports a luxuriously soft, thick, velvety coat and enjoys a diet of insect larvae and earthworms. A mole's lifespan is three years provided he steers clear of angry gardeners.

MOLE

Order: *Insectivora*

Family: *Talpidae*

Five to eight inches (12 to 21 cm) long of which around an inch (2 to 4 cm) is naked tail, the mole burrows beneath the surface of our lawns, beds and borders using powerful forepaws with long, sharp claws. Also a good swimmer, his mode of action through the ground resembles rowing, his broad forefeet acting as oars while his hind legs push him forward.

In spring and autumn the mole makes long, straight runs (surface runs) at a depth of 2-8 inches (5-20 cm), creating ridges in the soil and loosening roots of young plants which will die unless replanted. Not content with this, he leaves behind dirty great mole-hills as he goes along. Having compacted the sides of his tunnel walls using body pressure, he pushes soil up through the roof to the surface of the ground. These unsightly heaps mark the course of his run which he excavates at a surprising rate of up to fifteen feet per hour.

Surface runs may extend for as much as a mile and are used until the food supply is used up. Hungry moles will be tempted to eat tulip and iris bulbs as well as tubers and roots. However, the staple diet is earthworms and the mole has developed a fascinating technique for dealing with his prey. Having grasped the unhappy victim, the mole works his way towards the head end as if it were a piece of spaghetti. Being rather fastidious, he scrapes away loose earth from the worm's body and straightens out any kinks with his forefeet.

Mrs. Mole occasionally makes a quick trip from her 6-12 inch (15-30 cm) deep, grass- or leaf-lined nest to find food for her young. In spring she will give birth to as many as six blind, naked offspring after 30 days' gestation which leave home in five weeks, breeding the following spring.

Tunnel floors are smeared with the scent of male moles, discouraging other moles from sharing the tunnel. However, if the mole-run becomes vacant, a neighbouring mole will not turn up his nose at the opportunity to live in a prefabricated home.

Folklore would have us believe the mole leaves his tunnel once a year to take fresh air by daylight.

However, he has a plentiful supply of air in the earth and is more likely to come to the surface in search of drinking water during hot weather.

The larger the garden, the more difficult is the task of dealing with moles. Late winter and early spring bring a flurry of mole activity, although they are also busy at other times of year. The skills of rural mole-trappers are still much in demand and anyone with a large garden might wish to consider bringing in the experts.

There are two types of mole trap: the half-barrel trap and the caliper trap. These are placed in the tunnel by the mole-trapper and the unsuspecting mole is killed instantly as he passes along. The trap is examined daily and moved elsewhere if it fails to catch a mole within a few days.

Poisons, which are highly toxic and only available on license, should be avoided. Strychnine (from nux vomica seeds) is especially cruel, causing great suffering. Furthermore, if the mole dies on the surface of the ground and is eaten, the predator will also be poisoned. Many people are unhappy at the thought of moles being killed at all. In fact the Royal Society for the Prevention of Cruelty to Animals (RSPCA) recommends that gardeners learn to live with moles rather than resort to killing them. The mole soon establishes his main networks and so in time the appearance of new mole-hills will be much less frequent.

If you are very fortunate, you may even see the earth move as Mr. Mole goes about his secret business. Using a bucket and spade, you could deftly scoop him up, earth and all, and cart him off in the bucket. Transport him far enough and he will have no option but to set up home well away from your rehabilitating lawn.

If a mole catches a whiff of scent from a weasel, stoat or mink he is likely to make a quick diversion regardless of the fact that these animals do not specifically prey on moles. However, such scents are not commonly available and in any case would probably only be effective in a small garden.

Thankfully, moles also bring certain benefits since they recycle soil as they go along, mixing in rotting vegetation and leaves and bringing subsoil to the surface. This gives excellent material for planting and when added to well-rotted farmyard manure is wonderful when used for growing potatoes. If the weather is frosty, pour cold water on the mole-hill and go back next morning when it has frozen solid, lifting away the entire mound on a spade.

Their underground tunnels are also useful conduits for rainwater, thus helping irrigate fields and gardens.

10
TACKLING THE MOLE

The aversion of the mole to nasty smells has led to an abundance of remedies suitable for use in the smaller garden. However, since the mole sometimes returns when the smells have faded, some of the following methods should be regarded as short-term deterrents.

1. *Mole Smokes*
Mole smokes purchased from the ironmonger or garden centre soon let Mr. Mole know he is trespassing. These are placed in the mole-run and lit, allowing a heavy, sulphurous gas to permeate the tunnel network.

2. *Garlic*
Crush a few cloves of garlic and wrap in muslin. Pierce the ground several times to locate the mole-run then dig a small hole. Drop the garlic into the run and cover with soil.

GARLIC

3. *Creosote*
Soak a piece of rag with plenty of creosote and place into the mole-run as above. Do this at intervals along the run and replace every few days for maximum effect. It has been shown that creosote will not react with soil and so this method can be used quite confidently, although creosote should not come into direct contact with plants.

4. *Mothballs & Burnt Paper*
Further sources of noxious odours are *a.* burnt paper and *b.* mothballs made from camphor or naphthalene.

5. *Smelly Fish*

A lovely, ripe slice of rancid fish dropped into the burrow will repel all decent-living moles for a while.

6. *Paraffin*

Pour paraffin into tunnels as soon as surface ridges appear. Persist with this treatment and eventually the mole will circle around the treated area and away from the lawn.

7. *Elder*

If herbal remedies appeal, try placing a twig of elder in each molehill.

8. *Companion Planting*

Plant Caper Spurge (*Euphorbia lactea*) at 20 foot (6m) intervals around the garden as companion planting. The presence of this plant is believed to discourage moles.

9. *Mole-proof Bulbs*

Plant musky-scented *Fritillaria imperialis* (Crown Imperial) which moles and mice dislike.

10. *Diversionary Tactics*

If your garden is not too large, it might be worth attempting to force the mole into a diversion by placing a piece of slate at intervals across his tunnels.

11. *Scare Tactics*

Mowing the lawn with a petrol-driven mower is thought to scare off moles, perhaps by an overpowering combination of smell and vibration.

12. *Musical Deterrent*

Bury a bottle in the garden beside mole-run so that the bottle top is level with the soil surface. Moles move away from the sound made by wind blowing across the top.

13. *Subterranean Sound*

A battery-operated or solar-powered device comes attached to a stake which is pushed into the ground. This emits deep sound vibrations reputed to scare off ground rodents within 850 square yards.

14. *Ultrasound*

High frequency sound waves emitted from ultrasound devices used to ward off cats and mice might also be picked up by moles close to the surface of the soil.

15. *Rhubarb*

During the rhubarb season, donate a stick to your resident mole, placing it in the tunnel. He will not be too keen to use this tunnel again.

*

ACHILLES HEEL OF THE MOLE

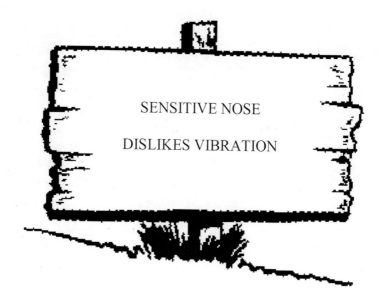

SENSITIVE NOSE

DISLIKES VIBRATION

EXPOSING THE MOUSE

This little rodent is better known as a domestic nuisance than an enemy of the gardener. However, although mice do not occupy all gardens, once they become established they can do a lot of damage in a short time.

MOUSE

Order: *Rodentia*

Family: *Muridiae*

In the wild, mice are just over six inches (17 cm) long including their 3 inch (8 cm) tail. Their coat is yellowish-grey with lighter grey beneath. Prolific breeders, they produce litters of five to ten young every ten to 17 weeks.

Mice have exquisite table manners, manipulating tiny morsels of food with their forepaws while nibbling away gracefully.

The celebrated *mus musculus domesticus*, the house mouse, tends to be larger than the wild mouse by virtue of the fact that he eats so much of our food! His unbounded appetite leads him to sample such delights as cheese, bread and all manner of fatty or waxy substances. However, in the wild, this animal is primarily garminivorous (grain-eating) but will also turn his attention to insects, nuts, fruit and small vertebrates.

Voles, short-legged with small eyes are brown/black with dark grey underparts. They will eat bulbs, roots and seeds and strip bark from young trees. Keep garden free of litter and mulches and use tree protectors.

MAN OR MOUSE?

One sure sign that a mouse is abroad in your garden is when you discover to your horror your precious seedlings nibbled bare at ground or compost level. He can also dig up and have a good feed on bulbs which have been planted close to the surface of the soil. An agile climber, the mouse will easily shin up bean stalks or find his way into precious pea pods and a hearty supper.

In the garden shed, evidence of 'a moose loose' includes mouse droppings and shredded polystyrene or plastic containers. Urine trails which fluoresce under ultra violet light help identify the best position for placing traps.

Since he can squeeze through the tightest space, any edible material left on the workbench provides a treat all too tempting. Mr. Mouse is very partial to a few seeds hibernating quietly in a cosy brown paper bag prior to germination. When this has happened once too often it is time to wage full-scale war. It becomes a question of.......

.... *MAN or MOUSE?*

*

*The best-laid schemes
of mice and men
gang aft agley*

Robert Burns

1. *Poison*

If you have a severe infestation, poison is an option but certainly not where pets or children are.

2. *Humane Traps*

Set humane traps (using bait such as marrow seeds) in sheds and greenhouses.

3. *Spring-loaded Traps*

 Spring-loaded traps can be used if you are a hard-hearted type of person. This task is made easier if we remind ourselves that mice are in fact disease-spreading rodents. Use cheese, oatmeal, bacon, or even chocolate as a bait.

4. *Sonic Device*

Ultrasonic devices are available which emit powerful high decibel frequencies harmless to humans and pets. Speakers direct the sound at either 180 or 360 degrees.

5. *Low-frequency Device*

Used indoors, this device emits a low frequency pulse unbearable to rodents and certain creepy-crawlies!

6. *Mouse-proof Bulbs*

If you are bothered by mice nibbling spring bulbs, choose some musky-scented *Fritillaria imperialis* (Crown Imperial) which they don't like.

7. *Chopped Gorse*

Lay chopped-up gorse branches around seedling bed.

8. *Cat*

Never fails.

ACHILLES HEEL OF THE MOUSE

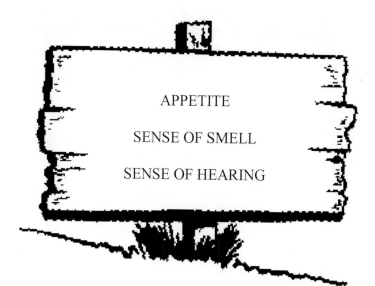

APPETITE

SENSE OF SMELL

SENSE OF HEARING

13
EXPOSING THE CAT

Just as bacteria cause infection when they find their way into the wrong place, so cats become enemies when they get into flower beds. Otherwise they play an important role in the well-being of their human companions and may well feel hurt to find themselves included in these pages.

DOMESTIC CAT

Family: *Felidae*

Genus: *Felis catus*

Short-haired cats are believed to have originated in ancient Egypt around 2500 BC and interbred with European wildcats. Weighing about 8 lb (3.6 kg), domestic cats are very flexible with over 230 bones (more than humans). They have powerful muscles using their tail to balance as they fall or jump. Cats mark territory by scratching, leaving scent from paw pad glands.

Cats have highly sensitive whiskers or vibrissae, sharp, retractile claws used for catching and holding prey and use their teeth for biting rather than chewing. Their eyes are adapted for night vision, they have keen senses of smell and taste and can hear even in the ultrasonic sound range. On average, litters of four kittens are born deaf, blind and helpless after 65 days' gestation.

Domestic cats learn by observation and experience, living for 15 years if they take advantage of their legendary nine lives.

Legally, cats are free to roam wherever the mood takes them, unlike dogs for whom owners can be held responsible for trespass and damage. Cats tend not to eat plants, only disturb or trample them, perhaps unearthing freshly-sown seeds or digging holes in seedbeds.

You can suspect cats when scratch marks and mounds of soil appear in newly-prepared beds. These mounds might contain faeces while scorched patches on the lawn could well be caused by cats' urine. Cats have been known to mistake a mulch of cocoa shells for a feline public convenience. Freshly-dug seed drills can be protected from cats by a wire cloche which will also keep birds away. Rose clippings can be inserted vertically into the soil as well as laid horizontally. Thorny material should never be placed at the bottom of a wall or hedge where cats are known to jump since this could cause painful injury to their paws.

*

Why was I born to be abhorr'd of man and bird and beast?
The bullfinch marks me stealing by, and straight his song hath ceased;
The shrewmouse eyes me shudderingly, then flees; and, worse than that,
The housedog he flees after me - why was I born a cat?

They call me cruel. Do I know if mouse or song-bird feels?
I only know they make me light and salutary meals:
And if, as 'tis my nature to, ere I devour I tease 'em,
Why should a low-bred gardener's boy pursue me with a besom?

C. S. Calverley
From:
Sad Memories

14
EDUCATING THE CAT

1. *Cat Loo*
Provide a patch with plenty of sharp sand or freshly dug earth in a remote area of the garden so your cat can dig a hole to use as a loo. Plant catmint (*nepeta faassenii*) nearby to attract cat's attention.

2. *Scratching Posts*

Cat owners might also choose to provide a wooden scratching post, preferably using wood that has not been treated although preservatives should be safe after a few weeks.

3. *Tree Guard*
Protect newly-planted trees with inexpensive spiral tree guards available from garden centres and nurseries. Made from recycled plastic, these black perforated strips last up to 5 years. You can also make your own from wire mesh and thick, perforated polythene.

4. *Raised Beds*
Discourage cats from disturbing vulnerable, delicate annuals by planting them in raised flower beds.

5. *Ultrasound*
Ultrasound emitters are popular cat deterrents.

6. *Mushroom Compost*
The discerning cat is offended by mushroom compost, tending to wander off in search of more fragrant surroundings in which to conduct his business.

7. *Thorny Warfare*

Sufferers from the uninvited cat often resort to serious warfare. Criss-crossed clippings from rose bushes, berberis or other thorny plants placed at strategic positions along the cat's entry route help him feel unwelcome. Spiky matting used to deter cat from scratching can be used too.

8. *Water Jet*

A sudden, unexpected scoosh of clean water from a washing-up liquid bottle can play a vital role in educating cats on social etiquette. A sophisticated variation on this method is triggered when the cat breaks an infra-red beam similar to a burglar alarm sensor.

9. *Reflective Deterrent*

Clear plastic soft drink bottles of water should be placed on their side in the flower bed. It is believed that sunshine reflected from the water keeps wary cats at bay.

10. *Luminous Eyes*

Paint the eyes of garden animals with luminous paint to imitate the eyes of predators which 'glow' in the dark. Only the bravest nocturnal intruder will wish to linger. Also imitation black metal cats with luminous eyes.

11. *Cocktail Sticks*

Place cocktail or kebab sticks upright amid seedlings.

12. *Repellents*

Proprietary pepper dusts, spray repellents, powder, gel, camphor and even orange scent are amongst the weapons available to desperate gardeners.

ACHILLES PAW OF THE CAT

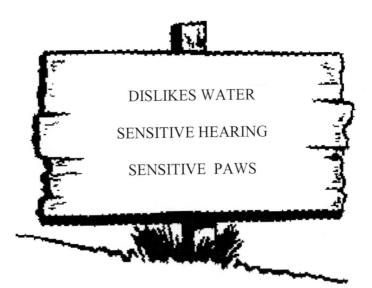

DISLIKES WATER

SENSITIVE HEARING

SENSITIVE PAWS

15

EXPOSING THE BIRD

The earliest known fossil bird is Archaeopteryx which lived around 150 million years ago and was about the size of a small pigeon. Birds inhabit every continent and almost every island in the world and are adapted to virtually every ecological environment.

BIRD

Class: *Aves*

The largest bird is the ostrich, 8 feet (2.5 m) high and weighing 345 lb (167 kg). The smallest are humming birds some of which are only 2.5 inches (6.3 cm) from tip of beak to tail tip.

Birds have keen eyesight and can perceive colours although they often recognise each other by their songs which use sound frequencies also heard by humans. A sense of smell is important only to a minority of birds and the fact that they only have few taste buds suggests that their sense of taste is not great either. Birds' eyes are especially sensitive to touch. They have a well-developed sense of balance and can detect the smallest vibrations.

Although mates may be associated for several years, the pair bond is renewed at the beginning of each breeding season. Plumage, which is important in this ritual also acts as camouflage and makes good insulation.

Birds would never win the medal as the gardeners' worst enemy. Indeed, many gardeners will be more concerned with encouraging birds into the garden and protecting them rather than fighting with them. They can be an asset in the garden so long as they content themselves with eating only caterpillars, grubs, insects and worms.

However, some will damage fruit and buds, even accidentally as they pick off aphids from young shoots. They eat seeds and berries, pull up onion sets and even steal plant labels. Overwintering brassicas (cauliflower and broccoli) are a favourite target of wood pigeons.

Therefore the behaviour of certain birds leads to many a headache for certain weary gardeners. It is handy to know which plants can be grown to attract birds and what can be done to dampen down their enthusiasm.

Most garden birds are attracted to elder, wild cherry, dogwood, berberis and cotoneaster. Grow these plants if you wish to encourage birds into the garden.

Since birds prefer yellow crocuses, plant purple or white ones. They seem to favour red berries so grow shrubs with yellow, pink or white berries. These could be yellow-fruited cotoneasters or viburnum, mountain ash, sclerodendron, callicarpa or snowberries.

Blackbirds which are attracted to seedlings in the cold frame can be diverted to safer quarters if you provide them with a seed tray full of wet mud mixed with grass.

Having ensured that seedlings and plants have been made as bird-proof as possible, soft-hearted gardeners might wish to salve their conscience with a few caring gestures. Indeed, the bird brings such joy to the garden that most people would rather risk the odd bit of damage in order to keep birds coming back to visit.

Serendipity plays its part too, since seeds dropped from the bird table have been known to sprout into beautiful flowers or even vegetables where they landed! As well as seeds, give grain-based foods (porridge oats and bread) and fatty scraps. Some birds, such as thrushes, are omnivorous and will welcome apple cores as a treat. Winter is the time when birds must be looked after on a daily basis, not forgetting some water in the morning.

If you have a garden pond, float a metal bowl or tin can on the surface and if the pond freezes overnight, fill it with hot water next morning. This gives the birds something to drink at the same time as allowing oxygen through to pond life. Bird tables, feeding areas and bird baths should always be kept clean.

Everyone knows that young birds in particular are apt to fly into windows. Unfortunately many have been killed flying into mirrors used as decoration. This should be borne in mind when designing or landscaping the garden. Dark bird silhouettes stuck on windows prevent accidents.

16
FLY AWAY, BIRD

1. *Netting*
Netting is expensive but an excellent barrier between bird and plant. Four inch (10 cm) mesh plastic netting will protect vegetable patches from pigeons. One inch (25 mm) will keep most birds away from fruit. 3/4 inch (19 mm) will exclude even small birds such as tits. Handy devices are available to connect cane supports. Check net frequently for birds, hedgehogs or grass snakes which may be trapped.

2. *Polythene*
Perforated polythene may be used in place of net.

3. *Fruit Cages*
Fruit cages made from aluminium covered with plastic netting protect soft fruits. Be sure birds are not trapped inside!

4. *Fleece*
Non-woven polypropylene 'fleece' designed as a cover for crops and fruit can also be used to keep birds away, giving buds a chance to develop into flowers.

5. *Scarecrows*
Scarecrows, glitter strips and noisy or shiny bird scarers are of limited value in deterring birds and should be moved around to prevent birds getting used to them. String a few aluminium food trays together and suspend above tomato plants or vegetable plots. These will reflect sunlight as they flutter in the wind, hopefully keeping the birds guessing whether it is yet safe to approach the area.

6. *Cotton Thread*

Nylon mesh or stakes with black thread criss-crossed between can be used to cover fruit and veg., but birds and hedgehogs can become entangled with distressing results. If crocuses are being severely damaged by sparrows, brightly-coloured cotton thread (which should be noticed and avoided by most birds) could be tried if all else fails.

7. *Canes*

Plenty of long garden canes pushed into the vegetable patch should prevent pigeons landing on your brassicas. Use canes around 5-6 ft (1.5 - 1.8 m) long.

8. *Bird repellent*

Commercially-available bird repellents are sprayed on buds to make them unpalatable. The success of this method depends on how hungry the birds are.

9. *Old Wig*

If birds spot an old wig hung on a tree or beside fruit beds it is said they might mistake it for a cat and keep well away!

10. *Distress Signals*

Recordings of bird distress signals have been used to keep birds away from the garden. Reports vary, but these appear to be only partially effective.

11. *Cat*

Keep a cat.

12. *Magpie Scarer*

Designed to scare magpies and raptors is an inflatable vinyl balloon with huge, round eyes and a reflective streamer. Does not worry smaller birds.

13. *Bird Saver*

The humane gardener concerned about birds flying into windows can purchase an adhesive vinyl silhouette of a diving sparrow hawk. Stick on window and birds will automatically fly away.

*

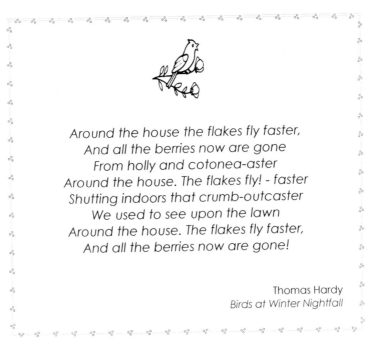

Around the house the flakes fly faster,
And all the berries now are gone
From holly and cotonea-aster
Around the house. The flakes fly! - faster
Shutting indoors that crumb-outcaster
We used to see upon the lawn
Around the house. The flakes fly faster,
And all the berries now are gone!

Thomas Hardy
Birds at Winter Nightfall

ACHILLES HEEL OF THE BIRD

SENSITIVE TO MOVEMENT

DISLIKES CATS

17
EXPOSING THE FOX

Foxes are found mainly in forests and deserts in America, Eurasia, and Africa. They adapt well to many climates and habitats, have short legs, an elongated muzzle, thick fur and a long bushy tail.

FOX

Family: *Canidae*

The red fox weighs around 15 lb (7 kg) and measures 36-42 inches (90-105 cm) in length excluding tail. His coat is reddish-brown with light-tipped hairs, paws and ears are black and he has a white tip on his tail. The fox lives for around twelve years and pairs for life, mating in mid-winter.

Two to eight cubs are born to the vixen in her den after 49-56 days' gestation. Their eyes are closed at birth and they are looked after by both parents for five weeks.

Solitary hunters, foxes can run at speeds of 30 mph (48 km/hr) but defend only small territories of 3 sq miles (8 sq km) since their prey is quite small. They eat carrion, rabbits, birds eggs, fruit, mice, voles and large insects.

Foxes can live near humans yet not be seen thanks to their alertness and keen senses of smell, hearing and sight.

18
OUTWITTING THE FOX

Foxes are an asset since they keep rodent populations down. They were actually introduced into Australia to cope with the plague of rabbits introduced previously!

Apart from the possibility that a fox might dig his den in the garden, he is likely to leave behind faeces and urine which will scorch the grass. Gardeners who also suffer from rabbits might be interested to know that fox urine is sometimes used as a rabbit deterrent! How the urine is collected is difficult to say. Foxes also eat rabbits as well as mice, rats, birds and insects. If you are unlucky enough to be bothered by foxes (this now applies to city dwellers as well as country), there are a few deterrents which can be used to scare them off.

*

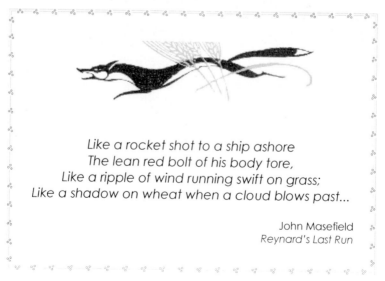

Like a rocket shot to a ship ashore
The lean red bolt of his body tore,
Like a ripple of wind running swift on grass;
Like a shadow on wheat when a cloud blows past...

John Masefield
Reynard's Last Run

1. *Lion Dung*

Clay pellets impregnated with liquidised lion dung are commercially available (see page 23) and can be spread around the periphery of the garden. Fresh lion dung can be supplied by the zoo.

2. *Phoney Predators*

Paint the eyes of garden animals with luminous paint to imitate the eyes of predators which 'glow' in the dark.

3. *Surprise*

Startle the fox into running away by the use of variations on the 'scarecrow' theme described in *Bird* and *Squirrel* sections. Anything producing sudden noise or movement can be tried.

4. *Ultrasound*

Ultrasound devices used for cats are also effective against foxes.

*

ACHILLES HEEL OF THE FOX

SENSITIVE HEARING

SCARED OF PREDATORS

AND

SUDDEN MOVEMENT

19

EXPOSING THE SHEEP

Sheep were first domesticated around 11,000 years ago in the area now known as northern Iraq. With numbers totalling more than one billion, sheep can be found in most countries of the world.

DOMESTIC SHEEP

Order: *Artiodactyla*

Suborder: *Ruminantia*

Family: *Bovidae*

Like the deer, these grazing, cud-chewing mammals are members of the order Artiodactyla which means they have even-toed hooves, supporting their weight on their second and third toes as they climb and run. Weighing between 165 and 440 pounds (75-200 kg), domestic sheep are up to 5 feet (1.5 m) long from head to tail with a narrow muzzle and pointed ears. They can live as long as 20 years and, after 150 days' gestation, ewes give birth to families of one to three lambs.

Rams have hollow unbranched horns which are larger and more curving than ewes' horns. Around 15% of sheep in the world are bred for mutton, including the familiar medium-haired breeds. Their teeth, which lack upper incisors, are adapted to chewing grass which travels through a four-chambered stomach for digestion. When they turn their attention away from grass and towards your plants, trouble ensues.

Only an unfortunate minority of people have to live with this menace. It could be argued that rural gardeners have so many advantages over their urban friends that why should they complain about a few sheep trudging their cloven hooves through the flower beds. The answer is simple.

To have a flower bed at all in the country is such a feat of imagination and patience that the unexpected arrival of an itinerant flock can bring on horrendous nightmares if not sleepless nights. Nor should anyone ever attempt to offer the usual advice to an insomniac country gardener: 'just try counting sheep'.

Imagine. You have read up all about rabbits; constructed nursery beds; planted perennial geraniums, shasta daisies, monarda. You have even read up about deer; planted shrubs and sprayed things. You're just beginning to feel confident when, as soon as your back is turned, a chomping great flock of sheep finds its way into your garden, making short work of your prize blooms.

Not only do they eat, they also trample all before them so that by the time the shepherd arrives with Fly or Shep, your beds are flattened and holed beyond recognition. The only ray of sunshine is the free pellets of manure they leave behind.

20
LIVING WITH SHEEP

Even the odd lamb in the spring can do a lot of damage. Speak nicely to the local farmer and see if he can add an extra couple of rows of wire to the fence (if you're lucky enough to have a fence between you and the sheep!) The expression 'battering ram' says it all: the forehead of a sheep is an excellent weapon against a weak fence. Observe a hungry lamb on a spring afternoon once he has spied your greenery. He will go on butting the fence until shoulders follow head through the gap allowing him to scramble out of captivity and into the freedom of your paradise garden.

The golden rule if you live near sheep is to keep them out by whatever means at your disposal. Even tubs which are high enough to escape foraging rabbits can be molested by sheep who will often uproot new plants such as heathers or cineraria, leaving them lying on the ground.

For some curious reason, sheep seem attracted to white plants but, so long as plenty of food is available, they tend to find certain plants less palatable than others. A selection of such plants is listed opposite.

28 PLANTS WHICH SHEEP TEND TO AVOID

*A*lchemilla mollis (**Lady's Mantle**)

*B*erberis darwinii (**Barberry**)

*C*alendula officinalis (**Marigold**)
Cistus purpureus (**Rock Rose**)
Cornus (**Dogwood**)
Cotoneaster
Crocosmia

*D*igitalis purpurea (**Common Foxglove**)

*E*ndymion hispanicus (**Spanish Bluebell**)

*G*eranium endressii (**Crane's Bill**)
Gladiolus

*H*ebe pinguifolia (**Veronica**)
Hedera helix (**Common Ivy**)

*K*niphofia caulescens (**Red Hot Poker**)

*L*upinus (**Russell Lupin**)
Lychnis coronaria (**Campion**)

*M*alva moschata (**Musk Mallow**)
Meconopsis cambrica (**Welsh Poppy**)
Mimulus (**Monkey Flower**)
Myosotis sylvatica (**Forget-me-not**)

*N*arcissus pseudonarcissus (**Wild Daffodil**)
Nepeta faassenii (**Catmint**)

*P*aeonia officinalis (**Peony**)
Potentilla (**Cinquefoil**)

*R*hododendron

*S*edum spectabile (**Ice Plant**)

*U*lex europaeus (**Gorse**)

*V*inca major (**Greater Periwinkle**)

ACHILLES HEEL OF THE SHEEP

THE RABBIT

The rabbit has a charming face:
Its private life is a disgrace.
I really dare not name to you
The awful things that rabbits do;
Things that your paper never prints -
You only mention them in hints.
They have such lost, degraded souls
No wonder they inhabit holes;
When such depravity is found
It only can live underground.

Naomi Royde Smith

67

21
A BRIEF LOOK AT THE RABBIT

The subject of unwanted rabbits in the garden merits a book all to itself* and so these pages give only a brief outline of tactics available to those under siege in a rabbit-occupied zone.

RABBIT

Order: *Lagomorpha*

Family: *Lepidorae*

Plants such as aquilegia, berberis, cotoneaster, forget-me-not, foxglove, iris, lady's mantle, lavatera, lamium, mimulus, and tradescantia grow happily in rabbit territory. But pansies, sweet peas, lobelia erinus, crocus and most annuals are fortunate to survive even one night.

So relentless is the rabbit once he has discovered a free meal ticket that many gardeners simply give up trying to outwit him and resort to increasing the size of the lawn or simply laying a patio!

However, there are ways of protecting precious plants, such as fencing, cloches, creosote and ultrasound. With some serious thought and plenty of determination, rabbits and gardeners can co-exist. If this were not so, the countryside could not boast so many splendid gardens. For gardeners driven to despair by the rabbit, help is at hand. Opposite is a list of plants known to be unattractive to rabbits in various parts of the country. Be inspired!

Gardening with the Enemy - A Guide to Rabbit-Proof Gardening by Janet Thomson (ISBN 0 9530013 0 X price £3.99) covers this subject in greater detail including a list of plants which rabbits love, techniques for protecting plants and ideas for seasonal planting.

Aconitum napellus (**Monkshood**)
Ajuga reptans (**Bugle**)
Alchemilla mollis (**Lady's Mantle**)
Anaphalis cinnamomea (syn. **A. yedoensis**)
Anemone coronaria 'De Caen' (**Windflower**)
Antirrhinum majus (**Snapdragon**)
Aquilegia vulgaris (**Columbine, Granny's Bonnet**)
Aster novi-belgii (**Michaelmas Daisy**)
Astrantia major (**Masterwort**)
Aucuba japonica (**Spotted Laurel**)

Begonia tuberosa (**Tuberous Begonia**)
Berberis darwinii (**Barberry**)
Bergenia cordifolia
Brunnera macrophylla (**Siberian Bugloss**)
Buddleja davidii (**Butterfly Bush**)
Buxus sempervirens (**Common Box**)

Camomile
Campanula medium (**Canterbury Bell**)
Ceanothus (**Californian Lilac**)
Centaurea montana (**Mountain Knapweed**)
Chrysanthemum maximum (**Shasta Daisy**)
Cistus purpureus (**Rock Rose**)
Convollaria majalis (**Lily-of-the-Valley**)
Cornus (**Dogwood**)
Corydalis lutea
Cotoneaster
Crocosmia
Cytisus scoparius (**Common Broom**)

Daphne
Dahlia hortensis (**Dahlia**)
Dianthus barbatus (**Sweet William**)
Dianthus (**Pinks**)
Digitalis purpurea (**Common Foxglove**)
Doronicum plantagineum (**Leopard's Bane**)

*E*chium lycopsis (**Borage**)
Elaeagnus pungens
Endymion hispanicus (**Spanish Bluebell**)
Epenedium
Eucalyptus gunnii (**Cider Gum**)
Euphorbia (**Spurge / Milkweed**)

*F*uchsia (**Hardy Shrub Fuchsia**)

*G*alanthus nivalis (**Snowdrop**)
Geranium (**all perennial varieties**)
Geum borisii (**Avens**)
Gladiolus

*H*ebe pinguifolia (**Veronica**)
Hedera helix (**Common Ivy**)
Hellebore
Heuchera sanguinea (**Coral Flower**)
Hosta (**Plantain Lily**)
Hyacinthus orientalis (**Dutch Hyacinth**)
Hydrangea macrophylla
Hypericum (**St. John's Wort**)

*I*beris umbellata (**Candytuft**)
Ilex aquifolium (**Common Holly**)
Iris xiphioides (**Dutch/English Iris**)

*K*niphofia caulescens (**Red Hot Poker**)

*L*aburnum watereri 'Vossii' (**Golden Rain**)
Lamium maculatum (**Dead Nettle**)
Lavandula angustifolia (**Lavender**)
Lavatera olbia (**Tree Mallow**)
Lonicera periclymenum (**Honeysuckle / Woodbine**)
Lupinus (**Russell Lupin**)
Lychnis chalcedonica (**Campion, Maltese Cross**)
Lychnis coronaria (**Campion**)
Lysimachia punctata (**Yellow Loosestrife**)
Lythrum salicaria Robert (**Purple Loosestrife**)

*M*alva moschata (**Musk Mallow**)
Meconopsis betonicifolia (**Himalayan Blue Poppy**)

Meconopsis cambrica (**Welsh Poppy**)
Mimulus (**Monkey Flower**)
Monarda didyma (**Sweet Bergamot**)
Myosotis sylvatica (**Forget-me-not**)

Narcissus pseudonarcissus (**Wild Daffodil**)
Nepeta faassenii (**Catmint**)
Nicotiana alata (**Tobacco Plant**)

Olearia macrodonta (**Daisy Bush**)
Oenothera missouriensis (**Evening Primrose**)

Paeonia officinalis (**Peony**)
Papaver rhoeas (**Field Poppy**)
Philadelphus (**Mock Orange**)
Phlox paniculata
Phormium tenax (**New Zealand Flax**)
Polygonatum (**Solomon's Seal**)
Polygonum affine / Persicaria affinis (**Knotweed**)
Potentilla (**Cinquefoil**)
Prunus laurucenasus (**Common Laurel**)
Pulmonaria saccharata (**Lungwort**)

Ranunculus aconitifolius (**Batchelors' Buttons**)
Rhododendron
Ribes sanguineum (**Flowering Currant**)
Rosmarinus (**Rosemary**)

Salix reticulata (**Net-leaved Willow**)
Salvia superba
Sambucus (**Elder**)
Saxifraga longifolia (**Tumbling Waters**)
Saxifraga umbrosa (**London Pride**)
Sidalcea malviflora
Solidago (**Golden Rod**)
Spiraea japonica

Trollius (**Globe Flower**)
Tradescantia (**Spiderwort**)

Ulex europaeus (**Gorse**)

Viburnum opulus (**Guelder Rose**)
Vinca major (**Greater Periwinkle**)

In *Gardening with the Enemy - A Guide to Rabbit-Proof Gardening*, a 'rabbit-proof star rating' system is used to help identify vulnerable varieties of certain plants. Each plant is described more fully including optimum growing conditions, soil type, description and size of mature plant.

In addition to the above plants, herbs such as chives, mint, oregano, sage and thyme may be grown in rabbit territories. Discovery of successful 'rabbit-proof' plants and shrubs is strongly influenced by local environment and conditions. This list of 105 plants is an excellent basis on which to experiment, saving time, money and patience by reducing the chance of buying plants which are doomed to certain failure.

*

The behaviour of animals can be modified to suit the gardener by the use of methods discussed in this book as well as by imaginative variations on these techniques. With the exception of strychnine used to kill moles, pest control is acceptable to the RSPCA so long as it is carried out properly and humanely.

Badgers and their setts are protected by law and so fences should be maintained to prevent them entering the garden. If badgers live in the garden, a license is required to persuade them to move on therefore the Department of the Environment, Food & Rural Affairs (DEFRA) must be contacted.

ACHILLES HEEL OF THE RABBIT

SENSITIVE EARS

SCARED OF PREDATORS

22
STRANGE BUT TRUE

When we have done all that is humanly possible to protect our gardens from the enemy, the best thing is just to sit down with friends and have a good laugh about them. Many good stories have come out of the garden and the following pages illustrate the humorous aspect of our common enemies.

Mrs. Macdonald of Ross-shire wrote, 'I am absolutely besieged with rabbits and have a Surrey friend who also complains of her garden looking like Colditz! We run to extra athletic bunnies here.....

One raider has been getting into my triple-fenced vegetable garden recently, but I gave chase a couple of nights ago. Before my astonished eyes it took a flying leap over the two-and-a-half-foot wire netting and straight through between two stakes of the outer chestnut paling! You have to admire such determination!'

Our family garden was visited one summer evening by a cow from the neighbouring field. Identified as no. 62 by her ear tag, this beautiful black and white Friesian found her way across the lawn, through flower beds and all the way up to the apple trees where she began to help herself to a free supper. Before the farmer arrived with Fly the sheepdog, no. 62 had sampled iris, monarda and aquilegia and looked set to tackle the rockery. As she ate her evening meal, the rest of the herd stood transfixed on the other side of the fence, following her every move with a loud accompaniment of worried lowing and mooing.

Next evening we were busy making necessary repairs to the lawn when a crunching of gravel alerted us to the seemingly impossible: no. 62 had returned for more of the same! More overtime for Fly. However, cows have been left out of this edition since there is very little that can be done about such an unlikely invasion.

Another farmyard escapee has been known to treat gardeners to a glimpse of ingenuity rarely associated with 'dumb animals'. Monica De Bremaeker of Ballater not only witnessed plants from her high window boxes being consumed by sheep standing on their back legs but new trees which had been fitted with protectors were also sacrificed in the most imaginative way. The sheep would sit on the the top end of the protector thus lifting the bottom end out of the soil. Once exposed, the poor tree would be systematically devoured from the bottom up.

Cindy Brookes of Staffordshire discovered a novel way to discourage starlings from the garden. Her pet rabbit, Misty, used to watch them out of the corner of her eye, pretending not to notice them. As soon as they descended on the garden she would chase them off.

The birds would perch on the fence and begin all over again but they eventually tired of being chased and flew off in search of safer surroundings.

Needless to say, Misty brought her own brand of mischief to the garden. She used to enjoy stealing fuchsias and petunias and parade around with them in her mouth, waiting to be chased by her owner.

A garden full of pet rabbits is a wonderful discouragement to unwelcome cats but the reverse is also true. Jennifer Walton of Perthshire has two young cats who get considerable delight from breakfasting on baby rabbits which can be dragged in through the catflap. Pet cats will also help protect the garden from damage by birds and squirrels.

Plant-loving pets seem to be smart enough to make themselves useful around the garden thus keeping their owners happy and their food supply flowing.

Not every gardener sees damage by animals in such a rosy light. While many enjoy a good chuckle and are unable to suppress a smile at the mention of rabbits and squirrels in the garden, some take a more sober view - especially those who earn a living from the land. It is surely forgivable for a farmer to opt for capital punishment rather than stand back and see his crops ruined. Thankfully the majority of plant-growers can afford to experiment with more imaginative methods while all the time enjoying the sight of these odd intruders in the garden.

Stories abound of squirrels going to hilarious lengths in order to steal from the bird table. Gardeners have been known to lie in wait for mole activity then strike with the spade just as the snout appears above the soil. One lady used to sit at an open upstairs window in the early hours of the morning with a shotgun, guarding her new young plants from rabbits.

Animals may be infinitely inventive in their quest for food, but a determined human can always find ways to fight back. As Mr. Burton of Jersey remarked, 'If all else fails, I can always throw the book at the little sods.'

*

Accuse not Nature
She hath done her part;
Do thou but thine.

John Milton

THE END

INDEX OF TOPICS

It faces west, and round the back and sides
High beeches, bending, hang a veil of boughs,
And sweep against the roof. Wild honeysucks
Climb on the walls, and even seem to sprout a wish
(If we may fancy wish of trees and plants)
To overtop the apple-trees hard by.

Red roses, lilacs, variegated box
Are there in plenty, and such hardy flowers
As flourish best untrained. Adjoining these
Are herbs and esculents; and farther still
A field; then cottages with trees, and last
The distant hills and sky.

Thomas Hardy
From:
Domicilium

INDEX OF EXTRACTS & ILLUSTRATIONS

ACKNOWLEDGEMENTS

For advice, inspiration and information, my thanks to Stanley Thomson, James Stewart, John Stewart, Bert Goodere, Alison Muir, Cindy Brookes, Monica De Bremaeker and Jennifer Walton.
For technical advice and assistance,
Clyde Computer Centre, Fullarton Road, Glasgow G32 8YL and Wells Computer Consulting Services, P.O. Box 30535, Oshawa, Ontario L1J 8L8, Canada .

                                                          J.T.

British Deer Society	01425 655434
RSPB	0131 557 3136/01767 680551
HDRA	01203 303517
Potato Marketing Board	01865 714455
Chemical Slug Controls	01473 830492/01992 623691
Biological Slug Controls	01932 253666/01233 813121
Ultrasound Devices	0870 544 9449
Solar-Powered Mole Device	0870 544 9449
Slug Traps	01453 511272/01483 273366
Electric Slug Fence	01967 402194
Electric Slug Saucer	01923 465410
Magpie Scarer/Birdsaver	0171 228 2360
Lion Dung Pellets	0870 544 9449
Capsicum for Birdseed	01545 590677

*

AVAILABLE FROM BOOKSHOPS & GARDEN CENTRES

GARDENING WITH THE ENEMY - *A GUIDE TO RABBIT-PROOF GARDENING*
by Janet Thomson   ISBN 0 9530013 0 X   Price £3.99
*
COMMON GARDEN ENEMIES - *A GARDENING GUIDE STARRING*
SLUGS, DEER, SQUIRRELS, MOLES, MICE, CATS, BIRDS, FOXES, SHEEP & RABBITS
by Janet Thomson   ISBN 0 9530013 1 8   Price £4.99
*
To order via the internet: www.rabbitgarden.com

To order from the publisher, please send cheque or postal order to:
Janet Thomson
5 Circus Place
Dennistoun
Glasgow G31 2JJ
Scotland, UK

UK customers please allow 50p per book for postage and handling
(£1.00 per book outwith the UK).

NAME (Block Letters)...
ADDRESS...
....
....

First published in Scotland in 1998 by

JANET THOMSON
5 Circus Place
Glasgow G31 2JJ
Scotland

First edition November 1998
Second Edition July 2000
Third Edition October 2002

Copyright © Janet Thomson 1998

ISBN 0-9530013-1-8

780953 001316

Published on SMS multi-media computer supplied by
Clyde Computer Centre, Clyde Business Centre,
Unit A4, Fullarton Road, Glasgow G32 8YL
www.GlasgowComputing.com

Published in Glasgow
Compiled by GEF Printers, 2 Camlachie Street, Glasgow G31 4JH

* * *